Copyright © 2017
Book Beetle Publishing
Melbourne, Australia
ISBN: 978-0-9954141-0-5

Written by Matthey Hartley
Illustrated by Lori Escobar

All rights reserved. No part of this publication may be reproduced in any form by any electronic or mechanical means including photocopying, recording, or information storage and retrieval without permission in writing from the author.

All events and characters portrayed are purely fictional and any likeness to any persons living or dead is purely coincidental.

Contents

The Scariest Monsters	6
The Clumsy Giant	8
The Intruder	10
The Terrible Transformation	12
Betsy's Hiccups	14
The Haunted House	16
The Mummy's Trip	20
My Troublesome Twin	22
Problem Pet	24
The Generous Granny	26
The Perfect Fit	28
My Zombie Teacher	30
The Princess In Distress	32
Mean Aunt Martha	34
The Wicked Witch	36
Valentine's Day	38
Franks' Fragrance	40
The Big Bash	42
My Mummy	44
Werewolf Woes	46

Matthew Hartley was born in Melbourne, Australia. From an early age he loved to draw and write, and dreamed of becoming an author when he grew up.

He wrote his first book in primary school, which was called Psycho Robots. He printed some copies and the book was a huge hit with his classmates, but it did not receive wider recognition.

Over the years Matthew has published humorous poetry, short stories and a children's book — Doodle & Sketch's Arty Adventure, about two unfinished drawings who want their creator to complete them.

In his spare time Matthew likes reading, gaming and, of course, writing.

You can connect with him on Facebook and also by email by writing to authormhartley@gmail.com

Lori Escobar is a digital and fine artist who refined her skills at the Maryland Institute College of Art in Baltimore, USA. She holds a BFA in illustration and a concentration in ceramics.

While Lori has multiple ongoing freelance projects in logo design and traditional painting (to name a few!), she works as an illustrator at Fifth Sun in Chico, California creating t-shirt designs and apparel.

In her spare time she paints murals and is also working on a stop-motion animation project.

You can contact Lori and see samples of her work at www.loriesque.com

A Fright in the Night and Other Rhymes

By
Matthew Hartley

Illustrated by
Lori Escobar

BOOK BEETLE
PUBLISHING

The Terror Of The Skies	48
The Hungry Monster	50
Pumpkin's Dream	52
Halloween Hunger	54
The Gargoyle	56
The Sad Skeleton	58
The Horrible Haircut	60
The Big Scare	62
Out On Halloween	64
Prediction Problem	66
The Headless Horseman	68
My Dad's A Vampire	70
A Fright In The Night	72
Hungry Horror	74
The Dragon's Birthday	76
The Eviction	78
A Monstrous Meal	80
The Foul Smelling Beast	82
The Scary Monster	84
The Terrible Task	86

The Scariest Monsters

I wouldn't want to see a ghost,
especially late at night.
I'm sure I couldn't handle it
as I'd get such a fright.

I think that vampires scare me too,
'cause they're the living dead.
To think about these scary beasts
has made me wet the bed.

Werewolves too, are frightening,
beneath the moon they prowl.
I know that I would jump in fear
to hear a werewolf howl.

All the monsters shown above
are really scary creatures.
But the scariest monsters of them all
would have to be my teachers.

The Clumsy Giant

I'm just a gentle giant,
but most would disagree.
Because when I've been spotted
they all decide to flee.

They yell, 'Here comes the giant!'
and raise the town alarm.
They just don't seem to understand
I don't mean any harm.

But people here are really small,
I squash them without knowing.
Mum says I should take more care
and look out where I'm going.

I told my Mum that I would try,
but still she wore a frown.
As soon as I had said those words
I'd knocked down half the town.

The Intruder

I heard my door creak open,
alone in bed last night.
Who was this intruder
that gave me such a fright.

I thought it was a monster
looking for a snack.
But I didn't want to be one
and decided to attack.

'You won't get me!' I shouted,
and leaped out of my bed.
Then I hurled my red toy truck,
'You hit my head,' it said.

It stumbled all around the room,
I heard it hit the floor.
'Have you had enough?' I said,
'or do you want some more?'

I fumbled for my bed light,
the intruder wasn't scary.
I wish I hadn't thrown my truck
and stunned the poor Tooth Fairy.

The Terrible Transformation

Today I saw upon my chest
that curly hairs were sprouting.
'I'm turning into a werewolf!'
I loudly started shouting.

Hair had started spreading,
which gave me quite a scare.
Hair was on my arms and legs,
hair was everywhere!

I didn't stick around to wait
for all the growth to grow.
If there was some kind of a cure
I really needed to know.

I hurried to my doctor
and made an awful scene.
He said, 'You needn't worry,
you're just a normal teen.'

Betsy's Hiccups

Old Betsy had the hiccups,
she had them day and night.
So Bertie thought it might be great
to give Old Bets a fright.

He lay in wait for Betsy
as she wandered down the street.
He leaped out from a bush and yelled,
'You're something I can eat!'

Bert thought that he'd succeeded,
scaring the hiccups away.
But when he smiled at Betsy
she'd nothing left to say.

Old Betsy had stopped hiccupping
and drawn her final breath.
Poor Bert had made a big mistake
by scaring her to death.

The Haunted House

Today I passed a creepy house
I noticed was for sale.
An agent standing out the front
was looking very pale.

He jumped right out in front of me
and then he grabbed my arm.
'Let's take a look inside,' he said,
'you're safe from any harm.'

I tried my best to wriggle free,
but couldn't slip his grip.
When we headed towards the stairs,
'Mind,' he said, 'don't trip.'

'I'm giving you a tour,' he said,
'of this family-friendly place.'
He led me through the open door
with a smile upon his face.

Soon I heard a ghostly wail,
I heard it loud and clear.
It curdled from the cellar
and filled me full of fear.

Then I looked at all the walls
and thought that I might faint.
They were splattered red with blood,
a crimson shade of paint.

The table acted strangely,
as it began to rise.
The agent told me I'd be best
to not believe my eyes.

He asked me if I'd like to buy,
but I of course said, 'No.'
He was looking quite upset
when I turned to go.

The agent told me then to wait,
he'd something else to say.
I wish I hadn't listened,
I should have run away.

He said, 'You're such a lovely guy,
I'll offer you a deal.
The price the house is selling for,
it's practically a steal.'

Although the house is haunted,
he explained it's quite unique.
Like a fool I was taken in
by his clever sales technique.

So now I own a haunted house
and living here is hell.
I'll need that real estate agent,
I think it's time to sell.

The Mummy's Trip

The mummy loathed his musty tomb,
which made him feel quite trapped.
He also wasn't happy
with how tightly he was wrapped.

It was very stressful
guarding the pharaoh's treasure.
He longed to do something else,
perhaps a week of leisure.

And so he went and caught a plane
to an island far away.
The vista was so beautiful
he wished he could stay.

He wore his speedos to the beach,
free from the daily grind.
After guarding the tomb so long
he needed to unwind.

My Troublesome Twin

I'm a two-headed ogre,
but I'm not like my twin.
We constantly fight,
he gets under my skin.

I know we shouldn't bicker
and I do not like to fight.
But we battle all day long
and also through the night.

No matter what, we'll lock our horns,
we never can agree.
Especially when it comes to choosing
programmes on TV.

We bump heads when I'm tired
and I say, 'It's time for bed.'
My twin has very different plans,
partying instead.

At tea we always squabble
about what's best to eat.
I'm a vegetarian,
but my twin likes eating meat.

When I play my music
he thinks each song is junk.
I love old classical music,
but he's in love with punk.

Arising in the morning
always makes me stressed.
We can't decide on anything,
not even how we're dressed.

Two heads are better than one,
that's what some people say.
But they would change their minds
if they were me for just a day.

Problem Pet

My monster pet refused to eat,
I did not know why.
So I thought that he should see a vet,
or he would surely die.

I rushed him to a clinic
and I said, 'I think he's ill.'
A vet came in to see him,
but he just would not sit still.

He jumped up on the vet's oak desk
and seemed a bit excited.
'He's full of life,' the vet exclaimed,
which made me quite delighted.

The vet exclaimed my monster pet
was not a vegetarian.
We soon found out his favourite food
was simply veterinarian.

The Generous Granny

Halloween's the time of year
I really do adore.
'Trick or treat,' the children say
and wait for what's in store.

'Skeletons and gruesome masks
could cause a heart attack.
Perhaps some treats will make you sweet,
wait here and I'll be back.'

I soon return with chocolate
and delicious hard rock candy.
And lots of gooey, gummy bears
I know will come in handy.

'Thank you!' say the children,
as I send them on their way.
Then I mutter softly to myself,
'I hope your teeth decay.'

The Perfect Fit

I hated being Big Foot,
it really wasn't fair.
'My feet are way too big,' I said,
'I've got no shoes to wear.'

But then I found a lovely pair,
imagine my surprise.
The left shoe slipped on easy,
it was the perfect size

I told the nice shoe salesman,
'I like the way it feels.'
Looking really shocked he said,
'But they are woman's high heels!'

'Even though that's true enough,
this pair I gladly choose.
It's not that often that I find
some perfect fitting shoes.'

My Zombie Teacher

When my teacher came to school
she freaked the whole class out.
'She's turned into a zombie!'
I soon began to shout.

She shuffled all around the room,
unable to converse.
She looked as though she might be fit
to ride inside a hearse.

Mostly she'd just stare at us,
her eyes were bloodshot red.
'She wants our brains!' I hollered
and half the classroom fled.

'You'll never eat my brain,' I said,
jumping up to fight.
But a coffee's what she needed,
she'd been up for half the night.

It only took her seconds
to scull the entire cup.
Then she looked herself again
and said, 'That woke me up!'

The Princess In Distress

The ogre caught the princess,
she needed to be freed.
I thought that I'd attempt the task,
so called my noble steed.

I galloped toward the ogre's cave
and clutched my pointy spear.
I smelt his foul and ghastly stench
and knew that I was near.

I walked inside his creepy cave,
where it was cold and black.
I had no time to light my way
and foil the beast's attack.

The orge tried to grab me
and squeeze me quite to death.
But I was much too quick and so
he drew his final breath.

I freed the lovely princess,
who batted smiling eyes.
She thanked me for the rescue
and said she had a prize.

She said I'd soon be knighted,
a thought I found appealing.
Until my teacher said to me,
'WAKE UP AND STOP YOUR DREAMING!'

Mean Aunt Martha

When my old Aunt Martha died
I thought that I was free.
She couldn't be mean to me anymore,
'cause she was history.

She used to steal my money for lunch
and delight in calling me names.
She'd also steal my father's sweets
and point at me to blame.

She'd kick my tiny sausage dog
and shred my comic books.
But what I hated most was when
she'd tease me 'bout my looks.

'You'll never, ever escape me,'
I'd often hear her boast.
Unfortunately she was right,
she's come back as a ghost.

The Wicked Witch

At night you'd often see me,
t'was then that I'd take flight.
And everyone that saw me
never witnessed such a sight.

I loved to ride my broomstick
to drag race through the sky.
I was the fastest witch alive
and taunted the passers by.

I felt so wild and fancy free,
the cool wind in my hair.
And when I crowed and cackled
I'd give them all a scare.

But now those days are over,
for speeding I'm grounded.
I lost my broomstick license,
so my vehicle is impounded.

Valentine's Day

We rushed to visit Mary,
to give her a Valentine.
But there was lots of pushing,
so she made us form a line.

Freddie's card was opened first,
then he got down on his knee.
Mary seemed quite flattered
when he spluttered, 'Marry me.'

Bill gave Mary flowers
and a poem he had written.
Mary said, 'Why thank you Bill.'
She seemed a little smitten.

She then accepted Teddy's gift,
a box choc-full of sweets.
It wasn't long before her face
was stuffed with tasty treats.

When she opened up my gift
her eyes were wide with fear.
She screamed out, 'It's a spider!'
How I love this time of year.

Franks' Fragrance

Frankenstein was hideous
and couldn't get a chick.
He needed a solution,
a clever, crafty trick.

He'd make a magic fragrance
the girls could not resist.
He wrote down the ingredients
on his shopping list.

He spent a lot of hard earned cash,
his perfume soon perfected.
His days were coming to an end
of feeling so rejected.

He found himself a subject,
a girl with lovely legs.
'Get away,' she soon cried out,
'you smell like rotten eggs.'

The Big Bash

Today I went to dinner,
for a massive monster bash.
The food was quite delicious,
I ordered potato mash.

Big Foot, sitting next to me,
was head to toe in stains.
I tried talking to the zombies,
but all they said was 'Brains.'

Some ghosts were at the party,
but couldn't eat the food.
When the waiter told them this
the startled man was booed.

A werewolf at my table
was very neatly dressed.
We told him that he must behave,
but he ate another guest.

The skeletons were hungry
and would not stop their eating.
A wicked witch ignored us all
and couldn't stop her tweeting.

The goblins made constant noise,
which made the waiter frown.
When climbing on the tables,
he yelled and said, 'Get down!'

The waiter then looked quite relieved
when Dracula said, 'Check.'
But when he hurried over
the Count just bit his neck.

The waiter tried, without success
to loosen Dracula's grip.
But then his day got even worse,
we all forgot to tip.

My Mummy

I'm proud to be a mummy's boy,
I think it's really great.
Some people like to tease me,
but I don't retaliate.

If you see my Mummy
you might be quite impressed.
She's not like other people,
– look at how she's dressed.

She let's me eat whatever I want,
and watch TV till three.
And even when I've been quite bad,
she'll never yell at me.

She really is the greatest
and she'll always stay that way.
Come to the museum tomorrow
and you'll see her on display.

Werewolf Woes

I always become a werewolf
when the moon begins to rise.
My clothes get ripped and torn
and then I double up in size.

Although I've got no clothes on
after I transform,
it's really not a worry,
as my fur will keep me warm.

When I'm a scary werewolf
out and on the prowl,
for awhile I'm happy,
you should hear me howl.

I really like to run around
searching for my prey.
When I find a tasty meal
they never get away.

But when I'm back to normal
it's really not much fun.
I have to get back home again
by doing a nudie run.

The Terror Of The Skies

It flapped its monstrous wings
and then it took to flight.
I knew I couldn't match it,
I'd never win this fight.

It headed right towards me
and swooped above my head.
And so I started running,
thinking I would soon be dead.

I made it to my little house
and quickly ran inside.
'Don't go out,' I shouted,
'if you do it's suicide.'

Mum thinks I'm overreacting,
I'll never fathom why.
There's nothing quite as scary
as an awful butterfly.

The Hungry Monster

A monster burst through our front door
searching for a feed.
We opened up the fridge and said,
'Take whatever you need.'

He cleaned out the fridge completely,
but the monster wanted more.
So he ate up poor old Wiskers,
who was sitting on the floor.

After that he looked around
and I saw an enormous grin,
as he gobbled up the food scraps
that we'd thrown into the bin.

But the monster wasn't done yet
and his eyes looked into mine.
I knew what he was after,
something else on which to dine.

'I wouldn't eat me!' I boldly said,
'it would be a big mistake.
But Mum's an unbelievable cook,
try her delicious cake.'

The monster greedily tried a slice,
but far from satisfied.
He wolfed down every single crumb,
then as expected – died.

Pumpkin's Dream

I have a dream this Halloween
to be a pumpkin head.
I'd sit upon the doorstep,
filling all the kids with dread.

I'd have a really creepy smile
and a candle burning bright.
I would look amazing
as my grin lit up the night.

When kids would come to Trick or Treat,
I think I'd start to talk.
And then I bet they'd run away,
too afraid to walk.

So that, you see's, my perfect dream,
except I have a hunch.
That I'm being put in a cooking pot,
I'll soon be soup for lunch.

Halloween Hunger

When I went Trick or Treating
I roamed a hundred streets.
So when I came back home again
I had a pile of sweets.

They all looked so delicious,
I just had to eat the lot.
I should eat in moderation,
but I guess that I forgot.

I scoffed down all the Smarties
and the giant chocolate block.
The candy took a while to eat,
as it was as hard as a rock.

I'd eaten all the tasty snacks,
(a very big mistake).
Cause I'm in bed at six o' clock
with an awful stomach ache.

The Gargoyle

I'm perched up high upon a roof
to give you all a fright.
I am a gargoyle made of stone,
designed to guard the night.

My eyes are red and piercing,
I have two spiky tails.
My teeth will cut through anything,
I'll scratch you with my nails.

I thought that I was hideous,
a gargoyle built to scare.
But I recently discovered
that some don't even care.

I am now a pigeon perch
and feeling very blue.
I wish I wasn't made of stone
and covered up with poo.

The Sad Skeleton

I'm just a lonely skeleton
with a plain old bony face.
I wish I had somewhere to fit,
but I just feel out of place.

My life was very dreary,
but it's boring being dead.
And now I'm feeling so depressed
I can't get out of bed.

And so I stare from wall to wall,
suffering my defeat.
I often wonder what to do
to make my death complete.

I'm staring in the mirror
and though I'm feeling shoddy.
I'm thinking I deserve a friend,
but I ain't got nobody.

The Horrible Haircut

My first name is Medusa
and I'm famous for my hair.
I went to get it cut today
and I got quite a scare.

'Can I have a trim?' I asked,
but the barber shook his head.
'Your hair is quite outdated,
let's try something new instead.'

And so he took his scissors
and soon began to cut.
I really didn't want to look,
my eyes were tightly shut.

When allowed to open them
I was quite appalled.
My slithery, slimy snakes were gone,
now I'm completely bald.

The Big Scare

I've nothing against my sister,
I guess that she's all right.
But wouldn't it be funny
to make her jump with fright.

At lunchtime when I spotted her,
I'd come along prepared.
I shared my big black spider,
but she wasn't even scared.

She said she quite liked spiders,
it was time to try Plan B.
I thought that it would surely work,
but had to wait and see.

I waited around a corner,
then jumped out and said 'Boo!'
But she just laughed out loud
and said, 'I'm not afraid of you.'

Determined still to frighten her,
whatever would it take?
And then I spotted at my feet
a vicious looking snake.

I hollered out a piercing scream,
my sister said, 'Fantastic!'
It seems that I'd been shrewdly fooled,
the snake was made of plastic.

Out On Halloween

The streets are filled with gruesome ghouls,
gurgling on the prowl.
And there's a scary werewolf,
with a loud impressive howl.

A crazy looking scientist
is acting quite insane.
A zombie keeps repeating that
he wants to eat your brain.

An axe murderer is also there,
hoping to get some candy.
And if he doesn't get his fill
his axe will come in handy.

Mum says, 'Go and join them,'
though I don't think that I can.
Cause she made me a silly costume
and I'm dressed as Peter Pan.

Prediction Problem

'You have a future dark and grim,'
the psychic said to me.
'I can't be more specific,
it's a murky mystery.'

'If you try to focus
it might just help you out.'
'And if you pay me more you'll find
I've more to talk about.'

I gave her all my hard-earned cash,
which made her really glad.
She peered into her crystal ball,
'This news might make you mad.'

I begged her, 'Tell me what's my fate?'
She whispered, 'Closer honey.
You can't afford the bus fair home,
because you're out of money.'

The Headless Horseman

The headless horseman went outside,
he'd heard the posties bell.
Although the day was bright and fine,
he wasn't feeling very well.

He opened up his mailbox
and he slowly reached inside.
But when he read his letters
the man abruptly cried.

'Oh no, whatever can I do,
my money's all been spent?
They're cutting off the power
and I haven't paid my rent.'

The headless horseman pondered,
'I'd not be in this strife.
If only I won the lottery
I'd get ahead in life.'

My Dad's A Vampire

My Dad's a scary vampire,
I know without a doubt.
I've heaps and heaps of evidence,
here's how I worked it out.

Vampires don't like getting caught
when the sun begins to rise.
So Dad sleeps soundly through the day
and at night he'll arise.

I also caught my Dad one day
drinking something red.
He claimed, 'It's aged red wine,'
but I was not misled.

I told my mother what I'd found,
she said, 'You're not that bright.
Your father has the graveyard shift
and has to work at night.'

A Fright In The Night

I found I couldn't get to sleep,
so flicked my bedside light.
Getting up to find a book,
I soon got quite a fright.

I froze completely with shock
at the monster I could see.
He looked so mean and really fierce,
but still I could not flee.

'You can't be real,' I said aloud,
as I rubbed my sleepy eyes.
But there he was as large as life,
a very big surprise.

I raised my hand above my head,
the monster did the same.
I thought that he was really weird
for playing such a game.

I asked him where he came from,
but the beast would not explain.
All he did was copy me,
which drove me quite insane.

Half hidden in the shadows,
his features far from clear.
His teeth all chattered loudly,
he was trembling with fear.

I offered him a chocolate,
to put him at his ease.
I cautiously approached him,
with weak and shaking knees.

I was shocked to learn upon
a very close inspection.
That the really ugly monster
was just my own reflection.

Hungry Horror

Luke, my friend, was famished,
he'd really lost his mind.
And so he reached out to eat
anything he could find.

First he ate a big green frog
and then a big fat snake.
I thought for sure that he'd be full,
but he wouldn't take a break.

He soon ate up some beetles,
with green and orange guts.
And when he ate some babies,
I said, 'Have you gone nuts!'

Then he burped a giant burp
and said, 'I'd like some more.'
The sweet shop owner blinked in shock,
'You've cleaned out half my store!'

The Dragon's Birthday

Donny was a dragon
who'd just turned eighty-eight.
His friends had all come over
to help him celebrate.

His Mum brought out the birthday cake,
everyone wanted a taste.
Chocolate was their favourite,
so none would go to waste.

Once the candles had been lit,
they sang the birthday song.
But after they had finished
it all went awfully wrong.

Donny wasn't concentrating,
feeling quite elated.
He blew a fireball from his mouth
and the cake disintegrated.

The Eviction

I had to evict a monster,
who lived beneath the bed.
I felt it time for him to leave
and go somewhere else instead.

I said, 'You won't intimidate me,
or give me another fright.
I've absolutely had enough,
you're leaving here tonight.'

The monster didn't move an inch,
he mumbled, 'Go away.'
I yelled, 'That's it! I'm quite fed up
and now I'll make you pay!'

I grabbed my math book from the desk
and whacked him on his head.
This only made him angry
and that was when I fled.

He chased me all around the room
and challenged me to fight.
And 'cause I'm not a coward,
I smiled and said, 'All right.'

Then I punched him on the nose,
but still he didn't flee.
He said, 'You must try harder
if you want to get rid of me.'

I grabbed a peacock feather
and let the fun begin.
The monster howled with laughter
and said, 'Okay, you win!'

And so the monster packed his bags
and went his merry way.
I knew that when my sister screamed
he'd found a place to stay.

A Monstrous Meal

I know a little monster
who was hungry for some tea.
And so I made him pizza
not fit for you or me.

First I took the pizza base
and covered it in grime.
Then I chose a slippery snail
and spread the base with slime.

Next I found some mustard,
the hottest of the hot.
Then I accidently sneezed,
and covered it with snot.

Next I added grated cheese
that smelt like stinky feet.
Then I put on slices
of some rotten, mouldy meat.

The yucky meal was heated through,
but still was undercooked.
When I checked the pizza out
I was shocked by how it looked.

The pizza just looked hideous,
I'd never make another.
I sliced it into quarters
and gave it to my brother.

The Foul Smelling Beast

Under my bed there's a creature
who's very mean and foul.
During the day and half the night
around my room he'll prowl.

I've put a peg upon my nose,
to help avoid his smell.
My bedroom used to be so great,
but now it feels like hell.

The beast when he is snoring
keeps me up at night.
And not a single day goes by
without the hugest fight.

At two a.m. he nudged me,
'Are you awake?' he said.
I'd like to trade my brother
for a better one instead.

The Scary Monster

As I was cleaning up my room
I got the biggest scare.
When I looked beneath my bed
I saw a monster there.

He stared at me with ugly eyes,
his back was slick with scales.
His feet smelt like potato skins,
his claws were sharp as nails.

The beast desired to eat me,
I tried to reach the door.
But someone must have glued me feet
and stuck them to the floor.

I truly thought my end was near,
but the beast began to plea.
He whimpered, 'Please be merciful,
don't eat me for your tea.'

The Terrible Task

Your little hands are trembling,
your knee bones knock and shake.
To open up this wooden door
could be a big mistake.
A foul disgusting creature,
behind the door it dwells.
With awful hygiene habits,
creating awful smells.
But there is something you must do,
it fills your heart with gloom...

You've finally been forced to clean your really messy room.

www.ingramcontent.com/pod-product-compliance
Lightning Source LLC
Chambersburg PA
CBHW080414300426
44113CB00015B/2511